Contents

What is an ocean? 4
What is a sea? 6
What makes the sea? 8
Moving water 10
Cold seas. 12
Below the water 14
Crossing oceans 16
Finding the way at sea 18
Fishing 20
Oil from under the sea. 22
Protecting the sea. 24
Enjoying the sea 26
Oceans around the world. 28
Glossary. 30
Find out more 31
Index 32

Some words are shown in bold, **like this**. You can find out what they mean by looking in the Glossary.

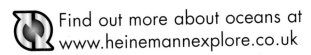 Find out more about oceans at
www.heinemannexplore.co.uk

What is an ocean?

An ocean is a huge amount of salty water that begins where the land ends. Oceans cover more of the Earth's **surface** than the land does.

My World of Geography

OCEANS

Angela Royston

Heinemann
LIBRARY

young
Explorer

www.heinemann.co.uk/library

Visit our website to find out more information about **Heinemann Library** books.

To order:

☎ Phone 44 (0) 1865 888066

▤ Send a fax to 44 (0) 1865 314091

▢ Visit the Heinemann Bookshop at www.heinemann.co.uk/library to browse our catalogue and order online.

First published in Great Britain by Heinemann Library, Halley Court, Jordan Hill, Oxford OX2 8EJ, part of Harcourt Education.
Heinemann is a registered trademark of Harcourt Education Ltd.

Editorial: Andrew Farrow and Dan Nunn
Design: Ron Kamen and Celia Jones
Illustrations: Jeff Edwards (p. 11, pp. 28–9)
Picture Research: Rebecca Sodergren, Melissa Allison and Debra Weatherley
Production: Duncan Gilbert

Originated by Ambassador Litho Ltd
Printed and bound in China by South China Printing Co Ltd

The paper used to print this book comes from sustainable resources.

ISBN 0 431 11799 3 (hardback)
08 07 06 05 04
10 9 8 7 6 5 4 3 2 1

ISBN 0 431 11804 3 (paperback)
09 08 07 06 05
10 9 8 7 6 5 4 3 2 1

British Library Cataloguing in Publication Data

Royston, Angela
Oceans. – (My world of geography)
1. Oceanography – Juvenile literature
2. Ocean – Juvenile literature
I. Title
551.4'6

A full catalogue record for this book is available from the British Library.

Acknowledgements

The Publishers would like to thank the following for permission to reproduce photographs:

Alamy Images pp. **18** (Boating Images P.L./K. Pritchard), **19**, **21** (Plain Picture/A. Biewer), **23** (Goodshoot); Atmosphere Picture Library p. **27** (Bob Croxford); Corbis pp. **4** (Massimo Mastrorillo), **5**, **9** (Jason Hawkes), **10**, **13**, **26**; Ecoscene p. **25** (Kieran Murray); Getty Images pp. **14** (Photodisc), **17** (Photodisc), **22** (Photodisc); Guillaume Dargaud p. **12**; Harcourt Education Ltd pp. **7** (Nicholas Beresford Davies), **8**; NASA p. **6**; Robert Harding Picture Library p. **16**; Science Photo Library p. **15** (Ron Church); Still Pictures p. **24** (David Woodfall); Wilderness Photographic Library p. **20** (John Noble).

Cover photograph reproduced with permission of Getty Images/Stone.

Every effort has been made to contact copyright holders of any material reproduced in this book. Any omissions will be rectified in subsequent printings if notice is given to the Publishers.

Large areas of land are called **mainland**. In most oceans, there are smaller bits of land surrounded by water. These are called **islands**.

islands   mainland

What is a sea?

A sea is smaller than an ocean. It is usually an area of the ocean that is partly surrounded by land.

*This photo of the Caribbean Sea was taken by a **satellite** high above the Earth.*

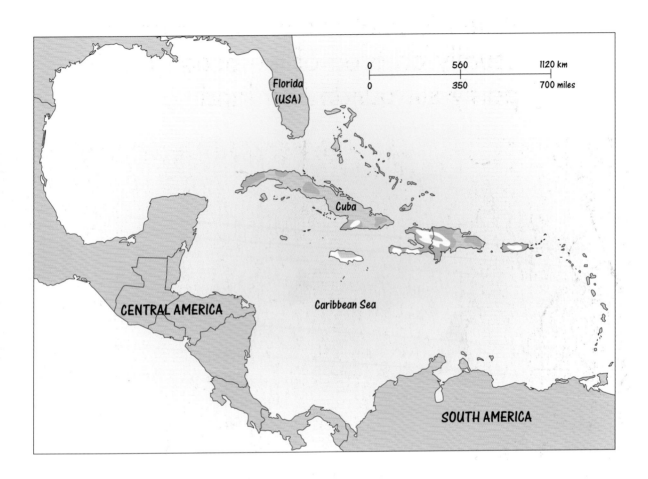

This map shows the same sea as the photo on page 6. On maps, the sea is usually coloured in shades of blue, even if it looks grey in real life.

What makes the sea?

Rainwater fills the seas and oceans.
Most of the rain falls straight into
the sea. The rest of the rain falls
on the land.

Rain runs off the land into streams and rivers. Rivers flow downhill and the water pours into the ocean or sea.

Moving water

The sea is always moving. Wind blows the **surface** of the sea and makes waves and ripples. When there is no wind the surface of the sea is flat and calm.

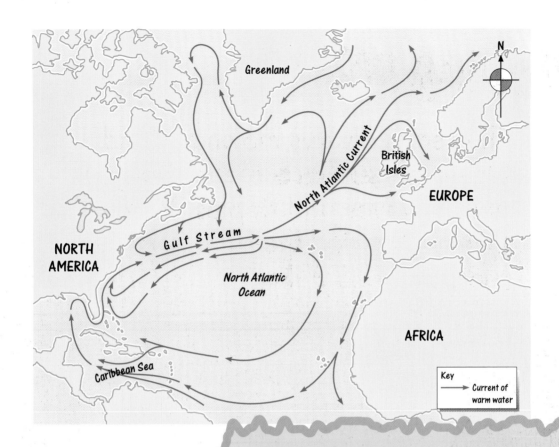

The Gulf Stream is a current that takes warm water from the Caribbean Sea across the Atlantic Ocean.

Some parts of the ocean flow like huge rivers in the sea. The moving water is called a **current**. Some currents are warm. Others are cold.

Cold seas

The North and South Poles are the coldest places in the world. The Arctic Ocean, at the North Pole, is so cold that parts of the **surface** of the sea freeze into solid ice!

Chunks of frozen seawater are called **ice floes**. **Icebergs** are huge blocks of fresh-water ice that float in the sea.

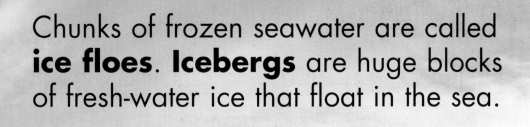

Ice floes are pieces of frozen seawater like these.

Below the water

The **seabed** is the ground at the bottom of a sea or ocean. **Divers** explore the seabed in **shallow** seas. Some divers look for treasure. Other divers study seaweeds and sea animals.

Most oceans are very deep. People
use **submarines** to explore the
deep water. They map the ground
beneath the sea.

Crossing oceans

Aeroplanes and boats carry people and **goods** across large areas of water. Many people prefer to travel by aeroplane because aeroplanes are fast.

*This ship is carrying goods in big **containers** on its deck.*

Most goods are transported across seas and oceans on ships. Many of the things we buy are made in other countries and then brought here by ship.

Finding the way at sea

Sailors can use a **compass** to help them work out which direction they are going in at sea. They also use maps called sea charts. Most sailors now use electronic equipment to work out where they are.

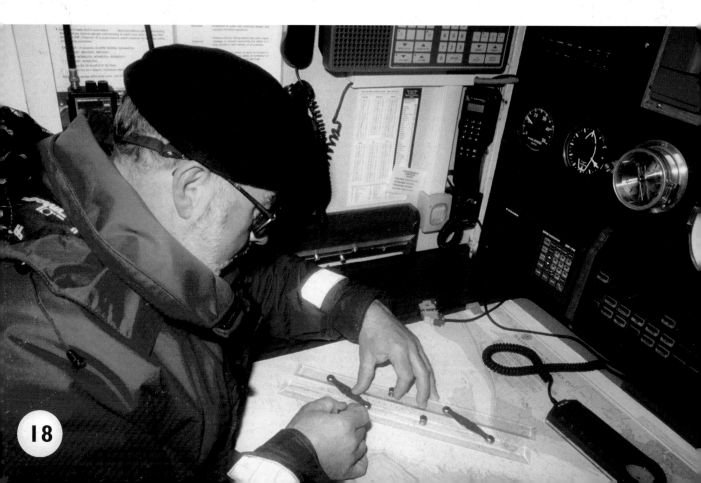

This sea chart shows part of the **coast** and the **seabed**. It also shows **islands**. On this chart, the sea is coloured blue.

Fishing

Some fish swim in seas near the **coast**. Others swim in deeper parts of the ocean. Fishermen use nets to catch fish for people to eat.

Fishermen drop nets into the sea
alongside their fishing boats. They
drag the nets through the water until
they are filled with fish. Then the nets
are pulled on to the boat.

Oil from under the sea

Oil lies deep below some parts of the **seabed**. People **drill** holes into the seabed to reach the oil. The oil is then brought to the **surface**.

Oil rigs drill for oil. This oil rig is in the North Sea between the UK and Norway.

Oil is taken to the **coast** along a long **pipeline** or on a ship called an **oil tanker**. The oil is then used for fuel or to make plastics.

Protecting the sea

The oceans are huge, but people are damaging them. Fishermen are catching too many fish in some seas and oceans. Some kinds of fish could soon disappear.

*Some fishermen use nets where the holes are too small. Young fish get caught before they can **breed**. This makes fish numbers fall.*

Some people pour **waste** into the sea. Sometimes oil spills into the sea by accident. Oil and waste kill sea animals. People should be careful not to **pollute** oceans and seas.

*This **oil tanker** has crashed into the rocks and oil has leaked into the sea.*

Enjoying the sea

Some people go on holiday on the sea. A cruise liner is a like a floating hotel. It has swimming pools, shops and restaurants.

Some people like to sail across the ocean in **yachts**. Sometimes yachts race against each other. They may have to sail through dangerous storms.

Oceans around the world

This map shows the world's oceans and some of its seas.

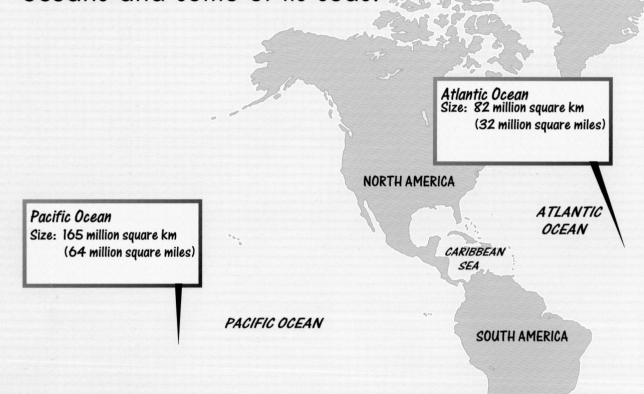

Atlantic Ocean
Size: 82 million square km
(32 million square miles)

Pacific Ocean
Size: 165 million square km
(64 million square miles)

NORTH AMERICA

ATLANTIC OCEAN

CARIBBEAN SEA

PACIFIC OCEAN

SOUTH AMERICA

 Find out more about oceans at
www.heinemannexplore.co.uk

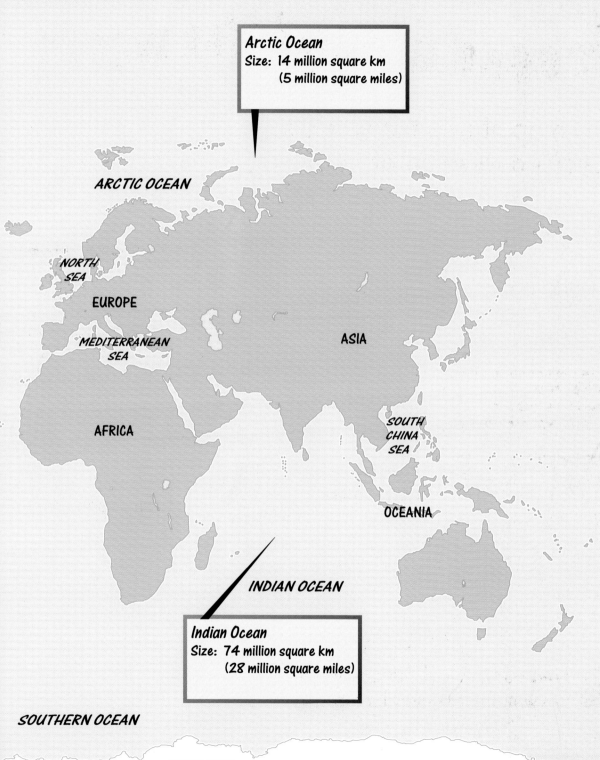

Arctic Ocean
Size: 14 million square km
(5 million square miles)

ARCTIC OCEAN

NORTH
SEA

EUROPE

MEDITERRANEAN
SEA

AFRICA

ASIA

SOUTH
CHINA
SEA

OCEANIA

INDIAN OCEAN

Indian Ocean
Size: 74 million square km
(28 million square miles)

SOUTHERN OCEAN

ANTARCTICA

Glossary

breed produce young

coast the land along the edge of the sea

compass an instrument that shows the direction of north

container a large metal box used to hold goods on a ship or aircraft

current a flowing area of water within the sea

diver person who swims below the surface of the sea

drill to make a hole by turning a long spike

goods things that are made, bought and sold

ice floe chunk of frozen seawater

iceberg chunk of frozen fresh water that floats in the sea

island piece of land that is surrounded by water

mainland land that is much bigger than an island

oil tanker special ship built to carry oil

pipeline many pipes joined together to make one long pipe

pollute damage something by making it dirty

satellite object put into space that can take photographs or send TV signals, for example

seabed the ground at the bottom of the sea

shallow not deep

submarine a boat that travels under the sea

surface the top or outer layer of something

waste left over materials that people do not want

yacht modern sailing boat

Find out more

Further reading

Eye Wonder: Ocean (Dorling Kindersley, 2001)

Go Facts: Oceans by Katy Pike and Garda Turner (A & C Black, 2003)

Make It Work! Geography: Oceans by Andrew Haslam (Two-Can, 2000)

Geography Starts Here: Maps and Symbols by Angela Royston (Hodder Wayland, 2001)

Useful Websites

http://mbgnet.mobot.org/salt/oceans/ – lots of information on the oceans and ocean life.

http://mbgnet.mobot.org/salt/coral/ – information about tropical oceans and coral reefs.

http://pao.cnmoc.navy.mil/educate/neptune/quest/quest.htm – this site has information about the ocean floor, ocean life, currents and waves.

Disclaimer

All the Internet addresses (URLs) given in this book were valid at the time of going to press. However, due to the dynamic nature of the Internet, some addresses may have changed, or sites may have changed or ceased to exist since publication. While the author and the Publishers regret any inconvenience this may cause readers, no responsibility for any such changes can be accepted by either the author or the Publishers.

Index

aeroplanes 16
animals 14, 25
Arctic Oceans 12
Atlantic Ocean 11

boats and ships 16, 17, 23,
    25, 26, 27

Caribbean Sea 6, 11
coasts 19, 20, 23
compass 18
crossing oceans 16–17
cruises 26
currents 11

divers 14

enjoying the sea 26–7

finding your way 18–19
fishing 20–21, 24
formation of seas and
    oceans 8–9

goods, transporting 16, 17
Gulf Stream 11

ice floes 13
icebergs 13
islands 5, 19

mainland 5
maps 7, 11, 19, 28–9

North Sea 22
North and South Poles 12

oil 22–3, 25
oil tankers 23, 25

pollution 25
protecting the sea 24–5

rainwater 8–9

sailors 18
sea charts 18, 19
seabed 14, 15, 19, 22
seas 6–7
submarines 15

waves and ripples 10

yachts 27